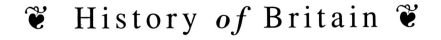
History *of* Britain

Tudor Children

Jane Shuter

Illustrated by John James

HISTORY OF BRITAIN – TUDOR CHILDREN
was produced for Heinemann Children's Reference
by Lionheart Books, London.

Editors: Lionel Bender, Sue Reid
Designer: Ben White
Editorial Assistant: Madeleine Samuel
Picture Researcher: Jennie Karrach
Media Conversion: Peter MacDonald
Educational Consultant: Jane Shuter
Editorial Advisors: Andrew Farrow, Paul Shuter

Production Controller: David Lawrence
Editorial Director: David Riley

First published in Great Britain by Heinemann Children's Reference,
an imprint of Heinemann Educational Publishers, Halley Court,
Jordan Hill, Oxford OX2 8EJ, a division of Reed Educational and
Professional Publishing Limited.

MADRID ATHENS
FLORENCE PRAGUE WARSAW
PORTSMOUTH NH CHICAGO SAO PAULO MEXICO
SINGAPORE TOKYO MELBOURNE AUCKLAND
IBADAN GABORONE JOHANNESBURG KAMPALA NAIROBI

© Reed Educational & Professional Publishing Ltd 1996

ISBN 0 600 58928 5 Hb   ISBN 0 600 58963 3 Pb

British Library Cataloguing-in-Publication Data.
A catalogue record for this book is available from
the British Library.

Printed in Hong Kong

Acknowledgements
All artwork by John James, except for maps by Stefan Chabluk.

Photo credits
Pages: 4 (centre): Bridgeman Art Library/Longleat House, Wiltshire.
4 (bottom): Bridgeman Art Library/Guildhall Library, Corporation of London.
5 (top): Fotomas Index. 5 (bottom left): Bridgeman Art Library/Sudeley
Castle, Gloucs - detail. 5 (bottom right): The Mansell Collection. 6 (top):
Museum of London - IT454. 6-7: By permission of the Trustees of The
Tate Gallery, London. 7 (top, bottom left): The Mansell Collection. 7
(bottom right): The Museum of London - 13566. 8: Bridgeman Art
Library/Kunsthistorisches Museum, Vienna - detail. 9 (left): Courtesy of the
Trustees of the V & A Museum, London - T134, 1928. 9 (right): Fotomas
Index. 11 (top left): Bridgeman Art Library/Musée des Beaux-Arts, Lille,
France. 11 (top right): The Hulton-Deutsch Collection. 11 (bottom):
Bridgeman Art Library/Wallace Collection, London. 12 (top): Museum of
London. 12 (centre right, bottom left): Fotomas Index. 13: The Mansell
Collection. 14: Bridgeman Art Library/Hermitage, St Petersburg, Russia.
15 (top): Bridgeman Art Library/Hatfield House, Hertfordshire. 15 (centre):
Museum of London - 5071/91/7. 15 (bottom): Bridgeman Art Library/
Kunsthistorisches Museum, Vienna - detail. 16 (top): Fotomas Index - detail.
16 (bottom): Bridgeman Art Library/Gilling Castle, Yorkshire. 17 (top):
Bridgeman Art Library/Fitzwilliam Museum, University of Cambridge.
17 (centre): Courtesy of the V & A Museum, London - T33, 1955. 18-19:
Royal College of Surgeons of England. 18 (centre): The Hulton-Deutsch
Collection. 18 (bottom left), 19 (top): The Mansell Collection. 21 (centre):
The Master and Fellows, Magdalene College, Cambridge. 21 (bottom):
The Royal Collection Enterprises/© 1996 Her Majesty The Queen.
22 (top right): Fotomas Index. 22 (bottom left): Museum of London - IT328.
22 (bottom right): Woodmansterne Publications.

Cover: Artwork by John James. Photos: Cradle - Museum of London. Boys
fishing - Fotomas Index. Boy holding nosegay - Bridgeman Art
Library/Wallace Collection, London.

PLACES TO VISIT

Here are some museums and houses that will give you some idea of what life was like for a Tudor child. Your local tourist office will be able to tell you about other interesting places to visit in your area.

Bethnal Green Museum of Childhood, London. Has a huge toy collection. Much of it is from a later period, but there are a few Tudor playthings.

Buckland Abbey, Yelveton, Devon. Francis Drake's home. Good for exhibits of Tudor daily life, and also has some of his things from his travels.

Burghley House, Cambridgeshire. The home of the Cecil family. Good for daily life of nobles.

Elizabethan House, Plymouth, Devon. Good for Tudor daily life.

Geoffreye Museum, London. Rooms from different periods that give an idea of daily life.

Highland Folk Museum, Kingussie, Scotland. Home life in the Highlands, shows how little life changed from early times until well into the 1900s.

Little Moreton Hall, Cheshire. Good example of 'black and white' (half-timbered) buildings.

The *Mary Rose*, Portsmouth. Ship sunk in the reign of Henry VIII, which has been raised and preserved. Ship and objects from it show what life was like on board ship.

Museum of Childhood, Beaumaris, Gwynedd. Victorian emphasis, but includes Tudor objects.

Museum of Childhood, Edinburgh. Mainly Victorian toys, but includes Tudor playthings.

Museum of English Rural Life, Reading, Berkshire. Shows how little country life changed over time.

Museum of London, London Wall. Various interesting exhibits, including children's clothes.

National Trust Museum of Childhood, Sudbury Hall, Sudbury, Derbyshire. Toys and displays.

Stratford-on-Avon, Warwickshire. Shakespeare's Birthplace, Anne Hathaway's Cottage, Mary Arden's House and Hall's Croft are all in and around Stratford. All give fascinating glimpses into life at the time.

Tudor Merchant's House, Quay Hill, Tenby, Wales. An early Tudor town house.

Victoria and Albert Museum, London. A few clothes, some furniture and tapestries and embroideries from the time. Also Henry VIII's writing case.

INTRODUCTION

What was life like for children in England in Tudor times? All Tudor children were expected to do as they were told. Babies were kept still and quiet. As soon as they could walk and talk, Tudor children had to start learning how to behave when they grew up. What they learned depended on how rich and important their parents were and if they were boys or girls.

It was a time of change and uncertainty. Disease struck suddenly, monarchs changed the religion of the country, rebellions broke out. It was also a time of new discoveries and inventions. The potato, tobacco and America were all discovered at this time, and the first printing presses produced books that allowed people to learn about the world around them.

CONTENTS

RICH AND POOR	4	
Coronation medal of Edward VI		
GROWING UP	6	
A baby's chair		
COUNTRY LIFE	8	
A bee 'skep', a basket-like hive		
TOWN LIFE	10	
Henry VIII, the second Tudor monarch		
PLAY AND GAMES	12	
Playing with a hoop		
HOLIDAYS AND ENTERTAINMENT	14	
Morris dancers		
READY FOR COURT	16	
Queen Elizabeth I		
LEARNING A TRADE	18	
An apprentice carpenter		
GOING TO SEA	20	
A Tudor merchant ship		
DYING YOUNG	22	
Surgical instruments		
GLOSSARY – DEFINITIONS OF IMPORTANT WORDS	23	
TIMECHART	23	
INDEX	24	

RICH AND POOR

"Children, obey your parents as the Bible commands and as they should obey their betters and all people should obey God," announced a pamphlet written in 1563. Children, rich or poor, were expected to do as they were told by their parents and by people who were richer and more important than they were.

▷ **Lord Cobham and his family, painted in 1567.** The lady on the left is his sister. Rich men who inherited the family estates were expected to look after the rest of the family – brothers, sisters, aunts, uncles, nephews, nieces and anyone else who was part of the family and needed support. They also had to look after the rest of their household – the servants and anyone else who lived with them and worked for them.

Most of the children of nobles lived in grand houses in the country. Their parents owned all the land around their homes. All the people who worked on the land had to obey their landowners.

Some nobles spent a lot of time at Court, with the monarch. The Court spent most of its time in London or in the royal palaces just outside London. But children were not welcome at Court. Courtiers' children mostly stayed in their families' houses while the fathers travelled the land with the monarch. These children rarely saw their fathers.

▽ **London in 1572.** Poor families lived in small houses. The rich lived in big houses with gardens by the river.

◁ **A gypsy family on the road.** They were called 'Egyptians' because of their dark hair and skin. This became shortened to 'gypsies'. They told fortunes or begged to make money. Their children learned to beg as soon as they could talk.

Not everyone lived in the countryside. Many people lived in towns, especially tradesmen who made things for a living. Most tradesmen's children lived at home until they were about ten, when the boys left home to learn a trade and the girls went to work as servants. There were many poor people. Their children had to work or beg from a very early age. They lived in the slum areas of towns, with many families crammed into badly built houses. In the country they lived in one-roomed cottages or in shacks in the woods. The very poorest families had no homes, and slept on town streets or under country hedges.

▽ **Henry VIII and, closest to him, his three children.** Kings needed children, preferably sons, to rule after them.

▽ **A family of beggars.** Some parents injured their children so they would earn more money begging.

◁ **Edward VI riding through London in 1547** watched by thousands of spectators. He was crowned king the next day, aged only ten years old.

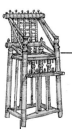

GROWING UP

Sickness and disease made life uncertain and quite dangerous for children in Tudor times. As many as six out of every ten babies died at birth. Out of every ten children that survived birth, two would die before they reached the age of 15.

Baby's cradle.

Babies were swaddled – wrapped tightly in cloths like an Egyptian mummy – as soon as they were born. Tudor childcare books said this helped arms and legs to grow straight. It certainly kept babies still and quiet. As they grew older the swaddling was left off and they learned to walk. As soon as they could walk they were dressed in smaller versions of adult clothing. From then on they were expected to grow up as fast as possible.

◁ **A baby is washed and wrapped up.** Tudor mothers had their babies at home. Childbirth was dangerous for the mother and the baby. There was not much that could be done to help either of them if things began to go wrong.

◁ **A Tudor cradle.**
Cradles were designed to keep babies safe from draughts. It was hard to keep babies warm in Tudor homes. Most cradles could also be rocked to help babies to get to sleep.

▷ **Death claims the child of a poor family.**
The first few years of a child's life were very dangerous. There were many more fatal diseases in Tudor times than there are now. Poor children were especially at risk. Their homes were cold, damp and draughty, so they were more likely to catch disease, and they were badly fed, so were less able to fight off infections.

△ **The Cholmondeley sisters, painted with their babies in 1600.**
The mothers and babies are in their best clothes. Under the fine material the babies are wrapped in layers of cloth bandages. These were changed sometimes only once a day.

Tudor families were larger, on average, than families today. Most families had at least four children. They might have many more. This partly depended on how many boys they had. It was especially important for wealthy families to have several boys who could inherit the family estates. They needed to have more than one boy, if possible, because so many children died young that it was safer to have two or three boys. Some parents even gave two of their sons the same first name, especially if it was a name they wanted to be sure to have carried on in the family.

This does not mean Tudor parents did not care for their children. They were more used to the fact that their children might die, but while they were alive they had the same concerns as parents do today. They bought their babies toys. They bought childcare books that gave advice on how to deal with toothache, feeding and minor ailments as well as problems of discipline.

◁ **A family discusses the Bible.** Children learned Bible stories, the Ten Commandments and prayers at an early age.

▷ **A Tudor child's woollen mitten** found in London. Most Tudor clothing was made of coarse woollen cloth.

COUNTRY LIFE

"Nowadays sheep do eat up men," Sir Thomas More, Henry VIII's minister announced in 1516. He was complaining that many landowners were growing corn instead of keeping sheep. This meant that they needed fewer workers on their farms.

The farm workers lost their jobs, and often their homes too. Their children were badly fed, housed and clothed. They had little chance to learn a trade to get a job when they grew up. Sometimes the whole family went looking for work. Children picked stones from the fields or helped with the harvest. But often the father left his family behind when he looked for work. If they had been thrown out of their home the mother and children often had to live in the woods. They lived off the food in the woods. The children had to pick leaves and berries, and learn to trap animals.

▷ **A busy country scene.** A rich man and his son are going hawking. Other children are helping their parents load sacks of grain for the mill. Some boys are playing football on the village green.

◁ (Far left) **In winter, food was scarce.** In this detail from a painting, hunters return from a chase and a child helps her family make a fire to burn off the hair of a pig killed for food.

▷ **Nobles hunt while the farmer takes his corn to the mill.** This is part of a Tudor table carpet (a heavy rug used like a tablecloth). The full-size picture shows all kinds of country people at work.

But there were many parts of the country where things did not change. The landowners still grew corn and employed lots of workers. The farm workers' children were made to work as soon as they were able to chase birds or watch sheep. As they grew older the boys learned to do other farm jobs, such as sowing, ploughing and helping with the farm animals. Girls learned to cook and clean. They milked the cows and made butter and cheese. At harvest time they helped in the fields.

Children of landowners did not work. Boys went to schools run by the Church, and learned how to manage their estates. Girls were taught how to run a large house with servants.

△ **Boys fishing.**
Children worked hard in the countryside from an early age, but it was also possible for them to have fun and find food for the family at the same time.

TOWN LIFE

"The number of carts and waggons and coaches is growing and the streets and lanes are so narrow as to make this dangerous," complained John Stowe in 1598. Stowe was an historian who lived in London, the fastest-growing town in England.

Most Tudor towns had traffic problems. The town centres were noisy and crowded, especially on market days. Many people kept chickens, maybe even a pig, in the yards of their homes, which added to the noise and smell. Towns were very smelly, for there were no drains or sewers and no rubbish collection. People threw their rubbish and sewage out onto the street. This was a nuisance, especially after dark, for there was no street lighting. But towns were also exciting places, especially for children. They could look at the various shops and listen to the cries of the people who walked around selling things.

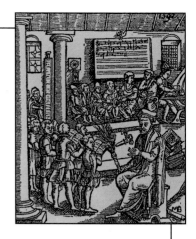

△ **A Tudor school.**
Some town schools were set up by the town council. Others were paid for by money left by local people in their wills.

◁ **A busy kitchen** in a town house.

◁ **A market scene.**
Children came to markets to buy food and household items for their parents. But markets were so full and busy that children could be a nuisance.

▽ **A boy holds a 'nosegay'** – flowers to sniff when town smells got too bad.

On market days in Tudor towns there was even more to see and do. There were stalls selling food, household things and even toys. Sometimes there were entertainers – acrobats, musicians, maybe even a man with a dancing bear!

Towns also had schools. Only boys went to school. Most people thought it was a waste of time to educate girls. They were expected to work as a servant or run their own home when they grew up. Those parents who thought girls should be educated either employed a private teacher, or taught them themselves. School hours varied. Some ran from 6 a.m. to 5 p.m. The schools that taught poorer boys ran for part of the day, so the boys could work for the rest of it. The main subjects were Latin and English. Pupils had to learn long passages by heart, and mistakes were punished with a beating.

PLAY AND GAMES

Tudor children did not have many toys, even those in rich families. The most expensive toys were carved and painted wooden dolls and ships from France and Holland. A girl from a rich family might own only one doll. But that doll would have jointed limbs that moved and lots of clothes to wear.

Children could still have a good time, even with few toys. In the summer most children spent a lot of time outside. The children of rich families learned to ride and hunt when they were very young. They played with hoops and balls in the gardens. They spent less time with other children than the children of poorer families.

All children played much the same games. Poor children had hoops and dolls and ships too, but they were less well made and less decorated. These toys could be bought at market stalls, or from pedlars who sold everything from ribbons to song sheets that gave the words and music to popular tunes. While poorer children did not have a chance to ride or hunt, they could go fishing, or swim in rivers or lakes, especially in the countryside. Along the coast, they could swim in the sea.

△ **A toy figure made from pressed lead**, probably by a blacksmith. Most Tudor toys were made from wood.

△ **Boys swimming in a river** in the countryside. Rivers in towns were often too full of rubbish, sewage and boats to be safe for people to swim in.

◁ **A Tudor illustration showing rich children playing** a variety of outdoor games and activities, including shooting.

In the winter there were different things to do. Cold and rainy weather kept most children indoors. Children from rich families amused themselves by reading, playing musical instruments or playing with cards or dice. They had a wider choice of things to do than poorer children, and also more space to play in.

Poorer children lived in smaller houses and had to make do with playing on the floor, on their beds or on the kitchen table. Very poor homes often had just one room in which the family had to eat, sleep, work and play.

But children did not stay indoors all winter, just when it was very wet. On windy days they could make kites to fly. In very cold weather there was snow to play in and ice to skate and slide on. Icy rivers could also be used for ice hockey and knocking over skittles with stones slid over the ice.

△ **Rich children playing outdoors,** watched by their parents. The older boys are playing skittles on the garden lawn. The younger boy has a spinning top. Children from poorer families played skittles using bones or logs as skittles and stones as balls.

▽ **Playing marbles.** Indoor games in Tudor times included marbles, dice, cards and draughts.

HOLIDAYS AND ENTERTAINMENT

"Every year at Shrove Tuesday the schoolboys bring cockerels and make them fight all morning. After dinner they go into the fields to play ball." John Stowe said this in *The Survey of London*, written in 1598. He was describing pastimes of Londoners.

People did not have holidays as we do now. The only time they had off work were the Christian 'holy days' of the year. Luckily, there were a lot of these days set aside to remember saints or events in the life of Christ. The most important of these days were Christmas and Easter. There were special church services and food and drink. On St George's Day people in almost every village in the country would get together to act out the story of George and the Dragon. Sometimes, travelling players would perform the show. Stowe says there were races and competitions in summer and boar hunts or bear-fights in winter.

▽ **A village fair.** Fairs were held on holy days.
● Musicians and actors entertained the villagers.
● People came from all around to join the fun. It got very crowded!

▷ **Fairs were not all fun.** If a person was not careful a pickpocket (like the one in the picture) might steal their purse.

△ **Rich girls playing music and singing.** Rich and poor people liked making music. The poor had to make their own musical instruments.

14

△ **A wedding feast in 1592.** At weddings, people ate, drank and danced a lot.

▽ **This painting from 1560** shows children enjoying games and entertainment.

◁ **People excavating a Tudor theatre in London** found these broken money box tops. Young children did not go to theatres, but apprentices and servant girls did. Large Tudor theatres held about 2,000 spectators.

Other sorts of entertainment for children depended on how rich their parents were and where they lived. Children of rich families living in the country might be entertained at home by actors. Groups of travelling 'players' toured England in the summer. Children from poorer families might see them perform at local markets and fairs. Children of rich families did not often join in village sports like football (played with no rules and often dangerous!) or ice hockey.

There was more entertainment in the towns. Only London had permanent theatres, among them the *Globe*, but actors came to towns more often than villages. Other performers also visited the towns – acrobats, singers, even 'snake men' with their exotic pets.

READY FOR COURT

"To ride, joust, use all weapons, run, leap, dance, sing and play all instruments tunefully, hawk, hunt and play tennis are all necessary for a courtier. Also he should learn several languages," announced Roger Ascham in 1570. Ascham was the tutor of Queen Elizabeth I and her cousin, Lady Jane Grey.

▷ **Queen Elizabeth I and a nobleman.** Windsor Castle is in the background. When the queen met ambassadors, her courtiers were expected to wait, out of earshot, in case she needed to talk to them for advice. If they wandered off at the very moment the monarch wanted them, they could risk being sent away from the Court or punished.

Noble girls were expected to learn less than noble boys. They could get by knowing some French, Italian and maybe a little Latin. Boys were expected to learn Greek, Latin, French, Italian and Spanish. Some books on education suggested that children should be taught Greek first, from the age of four! They assured parents that this was not too early – "for this is when they are quickest to learn, and after this all other languages will come easily". Noble children had to study hard. They had to be able to ride a horse because hunting and hawking were done on horseback. They also had to learn to sing and play musical instruments.

△ **Ladies of the Court** had to be able to play music, dance and sing well, but not as well as the queen! This frieze shows courtiers playing stringed instruments.

◁ **Hunting was a popular court pastime,** as here at Nonsuch Palace.

▽ **Noble ladies were taught to sew** and embroider. This embroidered elephant was made by Mary, Queen of Scots.

△ **A French dancing master teaches formal Court dances** such as the Almain. Before a girl was accepted at Court she had to be able to dance gracefully and well. She also needed to come from an important family.

Not all nobles' children could manage to learn all these things. Then they did not go to Court or went once or twice and were not noticed. Being noticed by the monarch was the quickest way to become part of the Court and to be given special duties or favours. But it was important not to upset the monarch, or other courtiers, by being too good at things.

Each monarch might be attracted by different talents or qualities. Henry VIII was most likely to notice a pretty girl with a graceful figure. Elizabeth I was quick to notice a handsome young man who could flatter her with poems written in a variety of languages.

17

LEARNING A TRADE

"Every child of six or seven learns a trade and so makes money for his parents or master," said Thomas Wilson, who wrote a book called *The State of England* in 1600. He added, **"Children from six to ten years of age working in Norwich have, in one year, made knitted stockings worth some £12,000."**

Children were an important part of the workforce in Tudor times. They were especially important because they made things without being paid a wage. A boy was taken on as an apprentice by a master between the ages of six and ten. He signed an agreement, called an indenture, with his master, promising to work for nothing as an apprentice. This was usually for seven years. In return he was fed, clothed, housed and taught a trade. Apprentices could work in all sorts of trades. Butchers, cobblers and bakers had apprentices. So did craftsmen in complicated trades like shipbuilding and clockmaking. Girls were not taught a trade. They worked as servants until they had a chance to marry.

▷ **Henry VIII meeting the most important Barber Surgeons** (doctors) in 1540.

▽ **A housemaid** dusting.

▷ **A clockmaker's workshop.** Skilled trades, such as making clocks, produced more money than trades like baking bread. Only boys from well-off trading families were likely to be apprenticed at this workshop.

◁ **A cobbler's apprentice** began work doing jobs like cutting out shoes from patterns.

△ **Masters did the skilled jobs.** Here, the tailor cuts the cloth; then the apprentices sew the seams.

Many Tudor children left home as young as six to begin work. Some apprentices and servants were treated well by their masters. They became almost part of the family. Many apprentices stayed on to work for their master after they had served their apprenticeship. If the master had no sons to take over the business, an apprentice could even inherit it.

Not all apprentices were this lucky. Some of them were badly treated by their masters. In the worst cases they were fed scraps, made to sleep on the kitchen floor and given old clothes to wear. Girls and boys were beaten regularly. They often ran away. If they were found they were forced to go back.

GOING TO SEA

Most Tudor children grew up to live lives that were like those of their parents. But a boy seeking adventure could join a ship's company. He could sail on trading ships or on vessels that explored new lands. He was sure of excitement and danger.

Boys could join a ship's crew at about ten, younger if they were big for their age. Many boys started by working on smallish ships called barques. These vessels sailed up rivers and around the coast of England carrying coal, wood or food. Barques had only a couple of crew. So if a boy was quick to learn, he would soon be doing most of the jobs on board. Boys on bigger ships were more likely to do boring jobs like scrubbing the deck and helping in the galley for longer. But they often had the company of other boys and made more exciting voyages.

◁ **Sailors furl the sails in bad weather.** Boys who did this job had to be good at climbing and have a head for heights! So did the boy on watch.

Most Tudor ships set out on trading trips, not voyages of discovery. They travelled to Newfoundland in North America for fish, Russia for fur, France for wine. They obtained these things on many occasions in exchange for wool, iron and salt rather than with money. Sailors travelled all over the known world in trading ships and faced many dangers. Trade routes had their share of bad weather, piracy and disasters.

A boy could sail off aged ten and not return until over a year later, when his family would hardly recognize him! It was quite likely he would never be seen again. Death at sea was common. Ships sank, sailors caught scurvy or fever, or were swept overboard in bad weather. One ship's log reported a lucky voyage to the Canary Islands "suffering no loss save for a ship's boy who was swept off the mast in rough seas".

△ **A busy port.** Some boys worked in ports rather than go to sea. Merchants needed help when they had ships to load or unload. Boys were cheap to hire.

▽ **An illustration from 1586 of a shipbuilder and his apprentice** drawing up ship plans.

◁ **Henry VIII's warships setting out from port.** Life at sea was dangerous for boys who worked on warships. The English were often at war in Tudor times, so ships could be caught up in battles and boys killed.

DYING YOUNG

Here is a rhyme passed down from Tudor times.
  "Ring a ring a roses,
  A pocket full of posies,
  Atishoo! Atishoo!
  We all fall down."
The falling down it talks of is dying from the plague.

One of the most striking differences between Tudor children and modern children is how much more likely a Tudor child was to die. Disease was a constant fact of life in Tudor times. Babies and young children were especially at risk. They were less sure of living long enough to become adults than children today. Children from poor families or those who lived in towns, or both, were most at risk. Most disease was caused, spread and made worse by bad hygiene, poor diet and overcrowded housing. Children continued to die young, from much the same reasons, until well into the 19th century. Their health improved only after the arrival of better sanitation, a clearer understanding of how diseases spread and the development of antibiotics.

△ **A brass memorial to Thomas Heron**, who died in 1517, aged 14. He may have been training to be a monk. A pen case and inkpot hang from his belt.

◁ **Herbal burners were used in Tudor sickrooms.** Many people thought bad smells caused disease. The posies (in the rhyme) were to prevent plague.

▽ **Memorials to two Tudor children** in 'Innocents' Corner' in Westminster Abbey. So many children died young that most were buried in unmarked graves.

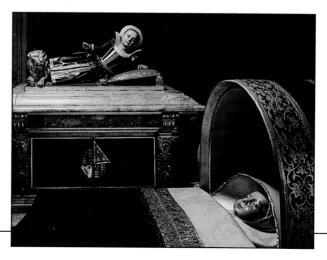

GLOSSARY

ambassador an official who represents his country while living in another.

apprentice a person learning a skill or craft from an experienced 'master'.

Court the monarch and the people who lived with and worked for the monarch.

courtier a noble person at court.

estate all the land and houses belonging to a particular person.

furl to roll up, usually with reference to a sail that is then tied to the beam that supports it.

household people who live with and work for the owner of the house and his family.

master the man who owned the house and was the head of the family. The master of a shop ran the shop and taught the apprentices.

memorial a statue or brass picture put in a special place, usually a church, to remember a person who has died.

monarch a king or queen.

noble a person from one of the important families in the country who had titles, such as duke.

pedlar a person who travelled around the country selling things.

saint someone that the Christian Church says has done something particularly holy.

town council the people who run the business of the town, often the richest and most important tradesmen.

trade can be used to mean either buying and selling goods or a skilled job (like baker or tailor).

will a document written by a person saying what they want to happen to their property and money after they die.

▷ **Map of Britain** showing the location of places mentioned in this book, including those listed under Places to Visit on page 2.

TIMECHART

1485 Henry VII, the first Tudor monarch, becomes king.

1509 Henry VII dies. His son becomes King Henry VIII.

1536 Henry VIII begins to close down monasteries and nunneries. The schools that these places ran close too.

1545 The ship, the *Mary Rose*, sinks off Portsmouth. All her crew, including the ship's boys, are drowned.

1547 Henry VIII dies. His son becomes King Edward VI. He is only ten years old.

1553 Edward VI dies. He names his cousin, Lady Jane Grey, as queen.

1553 Edward's oldest half-sister, Mary, becomes queen. Lady Jane Grey reigned for only nine days.

1558 Mary I dies. Her half-sister becomes Queen Elizabeth I.

1564 Birth of William Shakespeare, the play-wright. Boy actors played the parts of women in plays at the time – women were not allowed to act.

1584 The first English colony, Roanoke, set up in America.

1588 The Spanish send a fleet of ships (the Armada) to invade England. The English navy beats it back.

1603 Elizabeth I, the last Tudor monarch, dies. Her nephew, James Stuart, becomes king.

INDEX

acrobats 15
actors 14, 15 *see also*
    travelling players
ambassadors 16, 23
apprentices 15, 18, 19,
    23
Ascham, Roger 16

babies 3, 6, 7, 22
barques 20 *see also*
    ships
bear-fights 14
beggars 5
Bible, the 4, 7
books 6, 7, 16
bull-fights 14

Canary Islands 21
childbirth 6
Cholmondeley sisters 7
clockmakers 18
clothing 6, 7
cobblers 18
Cobham, Lord 4
country, countryside 4,
    5, 8, 9, 12, 15
Court 4, 16, 17, 23
Court dances 17
    Almain 17
courtiers 16, 17, 23

dancing 15, 16, 17
dangers at sea 20, 21
disease 3, 6, 7, 21, 22
dying young 6, 7, 22

education 11, 16 *see*
    also schools
Edward VI 5, 23
Elizabeth I 16, 17, 23
entertainment 11, 14,
    15
estates 4, 7, 8, 9, 23

fairs 14, 15
farms 8
farm workers 8, 9

fishing 9, 12
France 12, 21

games and sports 8, 12,
    13, 14, 15
    football 8, 14, 15
    ice hockey 13, 15
    skating 12, 13
    skittles 13
    swimming 12
    tennis 16
Grey, Lady Jane 16, 23
gypsies 5

hawking 8, 16
Henry VII 23
Henry VIII 17, 21, 23
Heron, Thomas 22
holidays 14
Holland 12
holy days 14
    Christmas 14
    Easter 14
houses and housing 4,
    5, 7, 8, 9, 10, 13, 22
hunting 12, 14, 16, 17

indentures 18

jousting 16

landowners 4, 8, 9
London 4, 5, 10, 15
    Londoners 14

markets and marketdays
    10, 11, 15
Mary I 23
masters 18, 19, 23
monarchs 3, 4, 16, 17,
    23
More, Sir Thomas 8
music 13, 14, 15, 16
musicians 11, 14

Newfoundland 21
nobles 4, 16, 17, 23

Norwich 18

pedlars 12, 23
pickpockets 14
piracy 21
plague 22
plays 14

riding 12, 16, 17
royal palaces 4
Russia 21

St George's Day 14
sailors 20, 21
schools 11
servants 5, 9, 11, 15,
    18, 19
Shakespeare, William 23
ships 20, 21
    ship's boys 20, 21
    trading ships 20, 21
slums 5
snake men 15
State of England, The 18
Stowe, John 10, 14
Survey of London, The
    14

tailors 19
theatres 15
towns 4, 5, 10, 11, 12
    councils 11, 23
    sanitation 10, 12, 22
    traffic 10
toys 7, 12, 13
trades and traders 5, 8,
    18, 19, 21, 23
travelling players 15

voyages of discovery 21

wages 18
weddings 15
wills 11, 23
Wilson, Thomas 18